# Buzz

Templar Poetry

First Published 2008 by Templar Poetry
Templar Poetry is an imprint of Delamide & Bell

Fenelon House,
Kingsbridge Terrace
58 Dale Road, Matlock, Derbyshire
DE4 3NB

www.templarpoetry.co.uk

ISBN 978-1-906285-26-5

Typeset by Pliny
Graphics by Paloma Violet
Printed and bound in Turkey

Templar Poetry Pamphlets
2008

**Amicable Numbers** — *Mike Barlow*

**That Water Speaks in Tongues** — *Siobhan Campbell*

**Lunch at the Elephant & Castle** — *Katrina Naomi*

**Yes, I'd love to dance** — *Maggie O'Dwyer*

Templar Poetry Collections
2008

**Admiral Fitzroy's Barometer** — *Pat Borthwick*

**Neurosurgery in Iraq** — *Rob Hindle*

**Walking the Block** — *Jane Weir*

**Unpredictable Geometries** — *Pat Winslow*

**Quarry** — *Dawn Wood*

# Acknowledgements

Acknowledgment is due to the editors of publications, in which several of these poems first appeared: *Acumen, Seam, Soundings, The Interpreter's House, Bridport Prize Anthology* and to magazines of which we may be unaware at the time of going to press. A number of poems in this anthology have also appeared among the winning and commended lists in several poetry competitions.

We wish to acknowledgment all the writers who submitted their work this year. Special thanks are due to Jane Weir, who was the Judge for the competition.

Templar Poetry acknowledges the support it receives from both individuals and organisations throughout the British Isles, the Republic of Ireland and beyond, and thanks are due to all who have assisted in raising awareness of the Pamphlet and Collection Competition.

Templar Poetry acknowledges financial support provided by Arts Council England.

# Foreword

The Templar Poetry Pamphlet & Collection Competition offers contemporary poets an opportunity to have their work published in pamphlet, anthology and collection form. Four excellent poets and pamphlets have emerged this year from the submissions, along with the work of poets published in the anthology. Poetry from thirty nine poets have work included in this anthology; a reflection of the excellent overall quality of work submitted.

Ten new Templar titles were launched at the 2008 Derwent Poetry Festival: four new poetry pamphlets and the anthology alongside four new full collections. The collections include first collections from Rob Hindle and Dawn Wood and new collections from recent Pamphlet and Collection Competition winners Pat Borthwick and Pat Winslow. Jane Weir's new work is an innovative poetic biography of the creative lives of two textile artists, Phyllis Barron and Dorothy Larcher. Readings by Templar poets ran alongside guest poets Paul Farley, Tim Liardet, Jane Routh and Jo Haslam.

Templar Poetry is committed to developing innovative modes of publishing excellent poetry and to developing audiences for new poets and contemporary poetry. Further information about Templar Poetry and its work is posted on our website, where full details of our list can be viewed. Our poetry publications can be purchased online and are also available from good booksellers.

www.templarpoetry.co.uk

# Contents

*Derek Adams*

## Exhumation

Normally it is the one dark place in a well-lit town
where only ghosts and cats roam, but tonight
among the quiet stone rows there is a digger
and a tent lit up like a big top,
police at the gates and cameramen outside.
Later when your black sheeted package
has been delivered to the pathologist,
when you've been winkled from your box,
placed on the stainless steel table
and he takes a surgical blade
in his rubber gloved hand
cuts from both shoulders to sternum
then down to the pubic bone,
peels back the skin to reveal the ribcage,
will he call the photographer over
"I think we'd better have a picture of this"
his eyebrows raised between mask and cap,
as he stares at the space behind the breastbone
at that cold black cavity that should contain a heart.

## Snow White

In the Mirror they call her a beauty.

Fine featured I'd say, it strikes me
every time I open the door to her.

Of course she looks a bit Goth
with her badly dyed hair and
the way her skin looks snow white
in the sudden cold light of morning,
almost matching the milk bottle
that I slip into the fridge.

Mind, she's not the looker she was,
I tell you when we first met
she had this glint in her eye,
smooth soft hands
and legs to die for
but that's all gone now.

I've taken her out once or twice lately
it's not the same though,
there is a coldness about her.

To tell the truth
I'm going to dump her soon,
why I've kept the around this long
I'll never know. Just sentimental I guess.
I'll take her out one more time:
a stroll down by the river,
run my fingers through her hair
then let her go.

It'll hardly come as a surprise,
for weeks they've been finding
bits of her body.

**The Gate**

This clear October morning
the frost just leaving the grass
and the ash trees a-clamour with rooks

I want to share
that the rowan berries are blood-red
and the leaves a sudden gold

to say these things are
ancient and brave – this year's
most tender saplings notwithstanding

& I am full of this hot chatter
like a rook seeking rooks
longing to spill out if you were here

> *only how still today is*
> > *and self-fulfilled*
>
> *even these derelict sheds*
> *no longer useful*
> > *grown beautiful*
>
> *where sunlight enters*

that makes of me a flat shadow
over the dug and undug plot
whichever way I turn —

stopping again to look
down the hill to the gate

knowing you won't come again

learning not to expect
to break the lock on the habit of it.

## Kitchen in Transit

My mother was knitting up a ravelled sleeve.
Everyone else in the flat was fast asleep
like dinghies in a creak-and-slop marina.
Small wet footprints shone on the kitchen lino.
A new view. Below: the casualty entrance,
the neon-lit triage nurse at her counter.
Beyond: black hills wearing necklaces of fire.
It was the twentieth century somewhere
between Merriweather by the Pacific
and One, Paradise Avenue, Mount Pleasant.
Elvis was entering his jumpsuit era.
A newspaper in a half-unpacked tea chest
showed an undrinkable boot-print on the moon.

Having made peace with the dust we depend on
for judging the relative distance of hills
or pointing at stars with powerful spotlights,
my mother was stepping through a proof, but then
she paused to doodle what were still considered
mathematical monsters: fern, cloud, coastline
– self-similar wonderforms inspiralling –
the night her three-dimensional dry-point print.

*Christopher Andrews*

## Continuous Screening

Hanging out the washing makes me watch the sky.
Slow pan over cinematographic cloud:
crumbling frescoes and collapsing parapets.
A background for near-enough-to-matching socks,
a T-shirt explicably fallen from grace,
faded to sky-blue pink and pegs weathered grey.
It may not be much of a drying day but
this is the sky I was born to live under:
split-level interiors intimating
the ghost-life that never seems to age (perhaps
because it's imaginary, which might mean
mine to assemble in imagination
from parts never meant to compose any whole

yet), full of activity, promising rain
to make me remember the shape of the roof,
to stipple beaches and percolate until
there can't be a dry corner left in the soil,
indiscriminate rain that falls all over
wedding plans and military operations
branded for cable news, precision hairdos
and the rubble of what was whole this morning.

# Mackerel

The Mackerel swims north above the bookcase.
His smell was ocean. His eye mica. His gills shut.
His scales glittered under the light. I tried to know him.

With a finger I traced the writing on his back,
dark blue, silver spaced. Runes. He belonged
in the grey cold of the North Atlantic
carrying the sagas of Odin, Thor, Njal and Iceland.

In the ice-packed tray on a market stall
this one finished his own first chapters – the shoal,
the nets, the hold, then paper shroud – my basket.
Unwrapped he lay vivid on the chopping board;
his body firm, his belly pale with a pink sheen.

In pencil that wouldn't show. I rubbed a shaded softness
I know is pink. Between finger and thumb I fanned
out his fins, opened his gills, pulled out the yawn
of his mouth, noted the lips, the stretched membrane,
imagined gulps of sea, gills working, then, the gasping.

I put him down on paper, captured his markings
his tessellating scales, his mouth, eye, gill, fins, tail,
his food-for-two body. Still he's going north
in his own mythology, in the dry dock of my wall.
But there's no knowing him.

**The Visit**

Helloes are wreathed in vapour.
The platform glitters frost. Mouths smile.
Eyes remain wary.
Her heart beats in disjointed jumps.

His orange hair blows in damp strands
across his cheek. The cheek she will kiss.

She huddles deep into her cashmere coat,
takes off a glove, stretches out her hand.

He stands stone-still.

She gently lifts the strands of hair aside
for her approaching face,
her mouth on unshaven skin.
He purses his lips, kisses the air
close to but not touching her scented ear.

"My train leaves in an hour or
the next is at ten?"
Her question mark hangs between them.
"Best have a quick sarnie then," he says.
"I've got a gig at eight."

## Feasting With Deirdre

More than anything, I long to take you out to lunch!
To Bellamy's, just along the Kennington Road.
We could stop in at the city farm first,
visit the chickens with stacks of feathers on their heads

like wigs, or helmets, oven mitts covering their spindly legs.
We could enter the church's garden for a minute's silence
to remember Margaret, then step into the glaring sun
before dodging into an alleyway as if we were in Jerusalem,

or Paris, and slip through the doors of the deli.
Over the counter, platters of blushed tomatoes and aubergine,
seas of baby leaves, goats cheese, grilled vegetable quiche.
Our mouths will be watering and I'll lean over

and say, *Choose anything. Everything!*
believing in all of those colours, that goodness.
Your skin will radiate health,
your hair grow back long and shining and sleek.

*Mara Bergman*

## The Part Fiona Played

She lived down the corridor, or we thought she did,
but maybe that was only DeLea. He was older,
wore glasses, his voice was high pitched
and they partied to Springsteen at all hours.

Littell Hall, Oneonta, New York, and this girl
from somewhere in England.
She wore skirts that flounced when she danced –
and she always danced first, had every boy swooning

though DeLea had already nabbed her.
We never really spoke, but she was my first
English person up close, fitting in
without even trying. She skipped classes, was always

hungover, but things somehow went right,
her accent gloriously spilling
while the rest of us struggled with work and with love,
the long winter days full of snow up the hill,

hair freezing those nights after swimming, arms aching
with loss. Last I heard she was living in California
and never looks back.

## Breast care nurse

She whistles in – flat shoes, primary colours,
wide surgical smile:

*Remember to take some softies when you leave,*
*use them as soon as your wounds are closed,*
*wear them with a comfy bra, baggy top,*
*nobody'll guess. Then call and make a date*
*for silicone ones, any size you fancy, they'll look good*
*under a T-shirt or vest. Try different brands*
*till you find what suits – so many kinds,*
*even stick-ons for nights.*

I want to tell her
I am my own woman-warrior,
heart just under the surface – I let go of pretence
weeks before the surgeon drew
his blue arrows on my chest.

**On TV**

Nigella wears burgundy velvet, a party dress
with plunging neckline, her black

black hair falls in ribbons over milky shoulders
down to full G cups. She demonstrates

the ease and desirability of flaking crab
with dill and fennel, coating little cakes

in egg and breadcrumbs, deep-frying plenty
to feed ravenous guests. She's so perfectly

convincing; I'm planning my own celebration –
champagne and sleep, the relief of a flat chest.

*Annie Bien*

## Pocket Sutra Unraveling Thought

Mother places the tiny sutra book in daughter's hand:
This was your father's. Your father's father, Dieh Dieh,
kept an altar in his closet. We all hid with Buddha during the war.

Dieh Dieh would sweep his five daughters into the altar, away
from the closet of white high heels ready to landslide
and the floral cheongsams. I happened to be standing

on the corner of Bubbling Well Road when the attacks
began. Your Second Aunt invited me in. Dieh Dieh prayed
some mumbo jumbo that I mimicked.

When I fell last week and hit my head on the ping-pong
table, you taught me a prayer from your Rinpoche. It's the one
we used to say, without Chinese accent. I never believed in religion.

But I never believed in not-religion either. Your father kept
sutras in his suit pocket. This one's very worn. He needed
it every day. I suppose it helped him. Language is a problem

when you have to leave your home. But now I can't even read
the signs that I know are supposed to be my language.
Keep these. Your father would be pleased. And take

this Buddha with the slim waist. Dieh Dieh said it was carried
across the Himalayas. The edge of the first page crumbles,
the second is torn, but you can still read the words Buddha said.

*Annie Bien*

## Hong Kong Baby

The Star Ferry scoots
with jaunty gait from Kowloon
to Fragrant Harbour.

Little Sour Bun,
Steamer Head, and Girl With Pearls,
pose for a photo.

My grandmother dubs
us with nicknames, chews my lunch
to a swilled mush, spits out
*Nai Nai Baby Pablum,*
and fills baby mouth with chopsticks.

This baby smells like steamed
white bread left on the kitchen counter
overnight. Yeasty.

Mother doesn't trust Nai Nai,
suffering mother-in-law syndrome.
Her own mother, Po Po, always
ranted about her worthless offspring.

Shut up baby.
You haven't even seen
how I had to dirty my face,
how I was glad I was plain,
how I missed my period
how my  toenails all fell off black,
how I hoped no soldier would grab me roughly
like that pretty Rose who was never pretty after.

Nai Nai wipes Sour Bun's congee lips:
Name her Peace and Prosperity.
Wish for her what you'd like to have
Wish for more.
Then she won't cry so much.

## Church

You waved away the guided tour,
side-stepped the welcomer. What you wanted

was to sit awhile in a beam of coloured light
just staring upwards. This church is like the one

you went to that night and found the vicar,
a dewdrop on his nose, digging a grave.

He said not to let the bats in,
wiped the mud from his hands

and followed you to the altar where you said
*I do* but it was only a rehearsal.

**Fit**
*(after Baudelaire's 'LesYeux des Pauvres)*

We answer to each other's names.

Your hand enveloped in my jeans back pocket,
mine riding the slide of the ridge and furrow
of ribs under your jacket.
Our strides walk in unison
effortlessly missing the cracks in the pavement,
divining daylight in the oncoming crowd,
swinging ourselves sideways as one of us
leads the way through.

We stop for a takeaway latte
we've agreed to buy without deciding.
My free hand fishing exact change
from your inside pocket,
yours sweeping up the cup from the counter.
Striding on, swigging coffee alternate.

A man, uniform, council green,
retrieving litter with a delicate claw
and in front of us and him an open mouthed bin.

I collide with you.

Miss the cup, never reach the bin I'm aiming for
as you drain and chuck the cup on the floor.

As we walk away I notice
how my shoulder is being nudged
in front of yours or pinned behind.

I can only remember my own name.

## Her Wedding Ring

She still wore it she said for our sake,
by which she meant, – though it went unsaid, –
we would not be called bastards even if he was.
So convinced had she been of its seal on their marriage vows,
they had argued after not before.

I never saw her wring it free
to throw at him like in the films.
It only came off when she threw pots,
replaced before the clay had dried
less she forgot.

And I don't know if she felt it cut in
beneath shopping bought after work,
with money he'd promised and she'd earned.
But she would often stop to change her grip
between the bus stop and our front door.

Years later when he rang they could talk
as friends without such history,
before she passed the phone to me, and after
she would smile and shrug in disbelief
at what she ever saw in him.

But she still tells of their adventures before,
when they camped their way round
thirty two states of America,
and people said they were so alike
they could have been brother and sister.

## Cellar

1940, but they feel safe here,
between the ping-pong table
and the bottled fruit.
Light from a tiny barred window
spills down dust-motes.
There's a birdcage
he always knocks his head on,
a cupboard that creaks.

Today it's hot,
they remove more clothes than usual.
Her buttons roll into mouseholes.
His braces, hurriedly unsnapped,
fly into a corner where they stay
for fifty years.
Upstairs, pans clatter.
*Where's Lizzy?* someone shouts
but with his tongue in her ear,
Lizzy doesn't cotton on.

Not knowing the way war will turn,
all their arrangements –
love tokens
sweat from their bodies

moons from their fingers
semen
salt —
lie in scuffs on the floor.

**Red**

'*Blood red or crimson?*' she asks, holding
up a sprig of berries. It's arts and crafts day.

We're making Christmas cards. She's on berries,
I'm on leaves. Pick and glue. Pick and glue.

'*I like this red,*' she says, '*Reminds me of a
pair of wellies I had when I was six.*'

The red she sees is her red, a one-off,
conjured up by her particular chemistry.

So much is taken on trust. Shared understanding
is nothing of the kind. I can never know her red.

# Jigsaw

A thousand pieces, each no bigger than
a tot's thumbnail.  Clouds of apple blossom,
an acre of thatch,  head-high hollyhocks,
a girl asleep in a hammock.

A day's work. Trial and error and trial.
Her carer stands behind her chair,
coat in hand, watching the clock.
Dusk presses at the window.

Nine hundred and ninety nine
small triumphs pressed home.
The last piece – the sleeping girl's slack face –
she sets this aside, orphaned in the box lid.

Our gentle anarchist. *'All done. Let's go home.'*

**Notice**

The May day holiday, and you bring home
redundancy, shrink wrapped, date stamped. We talk
of shock, or relief, opportunities

in disguise. We sleep, lie awake. Next day
the shower is blocked again and there are children
asking for bacon. Everything is the same,

and everything has shifted a little
to the left. We both cut out to sleep like failed
machines at odd times in the day. We talk

of how we might downsize. It rains. We lie
awake. By dawn, dandelions have punched up
like fists all over the lawn. Magnolias

are cupped hands catching something, or letting go.
You fix the shower, and discover a leak
behind the washing machine. We list our

next steps and hold hands. On Monday it pours
and we abort plans to cut back dead growth
or tackle the lawn. The crab apple stops short

of fizzing over. Tomorrow you will put on
your suit and drive to work as though anything
could change, and anything could be the same.

## The Water-Seller of Seville by Velazquez

A ring,
a cone of limpid light,
a glass goblet filled to the brim with cool water,
a fig to sweeten it.

The water-seller has come a long way,
kicking up the hot red dust of Spain,
his donkey tottering under the weight
of the heavy jars.

The city grills in the heat.
It smells of cooking oil and excrement.
Trussed chickens flap disconsolately
in wicker baskets.

The water-seller ducks into the cool room,
dazzled by the darkness.

Business is good.
A young boy approaches, a student perhaps,
his white collar crumpled
over his black doublet.
He stretches out his hand for the glass
which the water-seller balances, reverently,

between his thumb and his fingers,
like a chalice.

Hand to glass to hand the artist joins them,
drowsy, entranced.

*Susanne Ehrhardt*

## Growing up German

Growing up when the killing was over,
the dead tidied away, we knew our history
as electricity is known, by its effects:
fathers reduced to photographs,
dud bombs, American soldiers, refugees.
The rest came from books, much later,
and it didn't add up. So we asked.

When our fathers died defending murder,
how shall we remember them?
Where shall we shelve the pastoral,
hay wagon and willow pipes?
What are we to live by if we dare not
trust even your button collections
or the way you folded the sheets?

*Susanne Ehrhardt*

## Goose Wings

*Now she dusts the board*
*with a goose's wing*
            Seamus Heaney, *Mossbawn*

Your Irish mother's goose wing
sends me flying to a German barnyard
where the rooster rules the midden
under grandmother;
and I, her youngest and truest follower
scuttle after her
to the green-spattered goose pen.

She sets down
her hatchet, her steaming kettle,
bends from the hip and rises
wrestling the great white bird,
clamps it thrashing under her armpit.
She stretches the endless neck on the block.

She tells me to look away.

A spasm of webbed feet,
slackening.

Scalding water from the spout
slicks down the bluster.
Wet feathers drop by the handful
and the bird dwindles to its shocking gist
of limp, goose-pimpled nakedness.

She cuts deeply from ribcage to start
and names the yellow-flocked, glistening spillage:
'Darm', 'Leber', 'Magen', 'Herz'.

Later, two white wings hang to dry
from a nail on the barn door.
I stroke back the silky down
over the severed joints,
fingering the black scabs.

*Susanne Ehrhardt*

## First Death in Weiterode

That night, like every night,
grandmother sat on the firewood box,
hands folded over her apron.
She said she had laid out her brother.

That night, like every night
when it was time,
she creaked upright, sighed sleep-wells,
shuffled to her room.

That night mother scoured our hands
under the running tap, hissing
the stupid old woman
shouldn't have touched us
coming unwashed from a corpse.

That night in my cot,
I heard her squeaky quaver
'The lord's my shepherd'
behind the wardrobe
blocking the unused door,

and thought I heard,
threaded through her keening,
the death bird in the wintry apple tree
and closer, from the roof beam.

## A Drink With Camus After The Match

He wipes the ball clean
on the long sleeve of his jersey
flashing half a smile to me as he walks slowly off.
I'm igniting on the touchline
failing utterly to only half smile back.

He's changed in no time
eucalyptus burn of liniment
damp hair and soap cold skin;
laughing at the showers
which he says are primitive,
tepid long before he's rinsed.

He takes my hand and nods goodbye to everyone.
They tease him not to keep me out too late.
Across the round wood table
sticky with other people's drinks
he grimaces, as usual, at the beer.

I sip a fruit juice
spread my palm as if I'd brought the wings
which flashed across the garden earlier.
*Cinnabar moth* I tell him
*daytime flying, eats the ragwort.*

He smiles, diverted but not engaged.
I flutter in panic, spinning downwards
wishing *come back later,*
*come back when I know the things I'm going to know.*
*Kiss me when I'm deeper, bruised and complicated.*

Years later I rummage in his published notebooks
where bodies pressed against his skin
melt in the warm dark air
and find no mention of my name or this cold night.

When he kisses me goodbye
and asks me *Why so quiet? Why so sad?*
I try to say. He shrugs and wraps my words up
in the warm wings of his trench-coat;
tells me that I'm far too young to think so much.

*Maureen Gallagher*

## Why Should I Describe Sunsets?

When a trailer is towed to the rag-end of town,
to a site situated on top of a tip
where a swarm of flies mottles the sky
and seagulls drop pigs guts en route,

when in summer the smell from the nearby fill
permeates walls and windows and screens,
the vicious heat induces ennui
and there's not a blade of grass to be seen,

why should I describe sunsets?

When in winter the rats from the frozen heap,
flee to the huts where the children lie,
Richie's on tape singing *Aon Focal Do,*
the food's contaminated and a baby dies.

And the mother cries at the powers that be:
ye buffers think we're a different race,
the doctor sighs as he sips his Earl Gray:
woman, why do you live near waste!

Why should I describe sunsets?

When Mags and Tom go out for a night,
the City of Tribes slams a door in their face,
a juvenile beagle yelps in distress
back at the trailer, yards from disgrace,

and the councillor says: they're no better than dogs,

all they ever do is drink and breed,
lazy as sin, belly-up to the sun,
they have it too easy, they should be tagged like sheep,

why should I describe sunsets?

*Elaine Gaston*

## Walking to Marconi's

At first I think it is seaweed
the brown band that stretches from the shore
about half-way out to the island

all along the sweep of the beach
and on, to the headland.
Then I realise

it is the water from the river
high with run-off from the storm,
churned up mud and peat

that came sliding down from the mountain
into the glen
and made its way into the sea.

The stained waves hurl giant suds,
I know there is deeper green beyond.
The car door nearly blows off its hinges

as I step into the bluster
of early October. It is more like itself now.
It is the noise of the sea.

How could I have lived so long away
from the sound of it against the rocks
on one side, the chime of water down the hill

on the other, so long without
these broad flat blades of grass
that hold a single drop of rain?

I walk round to Marconi's
as fuschia hedges spill tears of god,
blackberries almost over,

first hazels in the scrub above
where we used to go for the scrog.
I count the beats between

the looms of the East Light,
wait for it to come round again
and again.

Then there is this bit of road
where the wall ends
and there is only air

between me and ocean.
Almost at Marconi's, when long low clouds
gather over the sound. I turn around

and reach the car
just as the island disappears
and the heavens open.

*David Gilbert*

## Sleeping with a balloon

We crept in to find the air
full of this whispering
that no rain, no car,
no night bird could explain.

The trees stood stock-still
at odds with this exhalation
like a toy train shoosh
or a thought that clings on.

We let our breath fall
to gather better its sigh
steady, defiant, like water
heading back towards the hills.

Then the headlights roamed
to sweep the room of shadows
and a momentary fire fixed
the source. We left him there

holding firm in dream.
We prayed it would not burst,
while we listened into the night
as it shrivelled in his arms.

## Search

Heat does it best; the smell of damp privet;
green breathes through the heat settled dust,
porch chequer-boarded orange and cream.
The third square along is still broken.
I've just stepped from the four-fifteen bus.
There's no sign of my brothers.

I squint through the glass; oblongs
of red, green and yellow pattern the lino.
The banister rail is still waxed.
I reach for my key but no need
when I float through the walls
pass cellar door, straight down the hall
and into the kitchen.  I search
for my brothers – the boys I took care of,
fought with, read to –

                    and it shifts in my dreams, a haunted
house with trembling walls; and I wake
with it so clear in my head I could touch
the door's flaking paint, the privet hedge
each oval leaf with its bead of rain;
the day before our mother left, my brothers
irretrievable men, still safe, fast asleep in their beds.

Jo Haslam

## Friday at Helme

Mod, you would have liked the joke,
your right-on cardboard coffin
like a giant pizza box. Nothing like that though
when she'd finished trimming it
with long kaffir lilies, late flowering cosmos,
your name on the side, Modwenna.

Mod, you would have been proud
of your daughter making it so beautiful
and your son, capable, taking everything in hand.

Mod, you should have seen Helme church
filled with your family, your friends,
everyone who loved you.

*Pamela Johnson*

## Ironing The Carrots

*I don't have time to iron the carrots*
clear self-talk inside my head.
I'm by the sink, holding a bag of organic,
scanning the sentence. Instinctively
I know *iron* is the faulty word.

Clearly I'm too tired to peel and chop;
musing on crossed wires, the brain's tricks,
I reach for frozen peas, surprised
at their warmth, register
I'm holding the sock-bag freshly tumble-dried.

My grandmother's voice floats up unbidden,
home after weaving her twelve-hour shift.
I lie down on the dining table, wrap
the white cloth around me and listen:
*I'm that tired I could sleep on a washing line.*

## Venetian Blinds

Horizontal lines of wafer-thin wood
suspended in a ladder of cords.
Was it really a Venetian
who configured this flexible geometry?
Not simply daylight to consider
but the sun's glare on water,
reflections flickering on stone.

Now, transcending its geography,
the device offers a way to negotiate: level
for brightness, close flat for dark, tilt
for every shade in between. You
never cared for them. They gather dust,
you said, are difficult to clean. You prefer
curtains. All or nothing. Open and Shut.

## My Japan

It began with the book on Japanese gardens,
where sand means water and rocks a mountain range.

In *The Unknown Craftsman* I read about potters
who made tea bowls and did not sign their names.

Wearing high platform shoes I clattered
over Hiroshige's Nihombashi bridge.

I sipped the reticence of *sabi* and the hot water
of *wabi* in *The Book of Tea* by Okakura.

Tanizaki's *In Praise of Shadows* lifted the lid
of a lacquered dish to the gleam of white rice pearls.

But it was Basho's haiku *Matsushima*
that propelled me to those pine islands in the north.

He thought the bay so beautiful the only words
he needed were the name and ... 'Ah!'

## A Man I Slightly Know

We share the arm between the seats.
Our breathing sometimes coincides
and we are conscious of a closeness
in the absence of our mutual friend.

It can't do much harm to flirt a little –
*Prenderò quel brunettino* Dorabella sings,
her sister Fiordiligi will take the fair one –
they anticipate the joys ahead.

We hardly know each other and in silence
communicate, now and then, discomfort
at too intimate a touch. We shift
position. One of us surrenders the arm.

## Dog-Day Afternoon

Damp heat and thick silence;
bird-movement minimal – just
butterflies, haphazard, diligent.

My baby, in her long-legged basket,
sleeps on the verandah – shaded by blossom
and drugged with the scent of frangipani.

She does not stir at the rifle-cracks I recognise
from elsewhere, pictures deep-imprinted.  I leave Lucy,
pelt across wide space to next door's empty bungalow.

Too late.  No silence here – white-walled verandah
splashed with blood, three pups already dead
and the bitch, shot through the belly, screaming.

I shout at them, two startled Tamils, one Malay
who holds the gun.  I stretch for it – try
to make him finish her – he shies back

from me: white woman, ranting gibberish –
wilder than the bitch?  I've no words
to tell them all I want is her quick death.

They stare – somehow get a rope around her neck,
drag her, writhing and half-choked, inside their truck;
doors slam, they drive away. The air grows quiet.

Lucy is still sleeping. The red of bougainvillea
hangs safely over her. One mason-wasp
explores the whiteness of our wall.

*John Mackay*

## Unseen

*Get your head down, son.* The words
that punctuated weekday mornings
as I reluctantly pulled on my coat.
*Then you can hold your head high
when you leave.*

          That afternoon at school,
an incident: four boys onto one
in the showers when he had his back
turned. Naked and glasses-less,
he fought for footing in the scummy
water as they reddened his slithering
ribs with their knuckles. Then
scuffled him into his blazer
and to the hooks, to hang like a rack
of lamb. His face in flames, a string
of blood and snot dangling from his chin.

*I saw nothing, sir.* The words
I rehearsed as my friend lay bruised,
too petrified to sleep in his own bed.
*It must have happened after I left.*

*Simone Mansell Broome*

# Pixie boots

I ask you what you can still picture...
*Pixie boots* you say. You say I was wearing pixie boots
and that I took them off at the water's edge,
so we could paddle that grey Autumn afternoon.

You say it was sunny; I recall only a dull day,
neither stormy nor bright nor bitterly cold,
the sun just trying, now and then,
to break through and make a difference.

You talk of lunch – a chav caff – stewed tea
and jacket spuds with beans or cheese or both.
*I'm going to make that be some other day.* And
as for pixie boots, well I can see the heels,

but there's nothing too pointy or elvish, and I
had packed sensible footwear...we were just
in too much haste to reach that tired slice of shingle,
*(only a breath between tussock and graphite sea)*

for me to change shoes first. You mention
the bleached wooden pallet, you licking and
sucking and drying my salty feet, both blind to
beachcombers, dogwalkers and passersby.

Let's agree on that flotsam pallet, the sand in my hair,
the kissing of toes. But I think the weather may've turned,
that perhaps we rushed back, ran for shelter,
spent a long afternoon listening to the rain.

**Fairy Tale**

He has found Goldilocks and the Three Bears.
While we eat, his daddy tells him the story.
At the end he beams with happiness
and says, "I love you, Daddy!"
"And I love you," says his daddy.
He says, "I love you, Mummy!"
"And I love you," says his mummy.
He goes on, porridge bowl overflowing,
"And Daddy loves Mummy!"
His mummy finishes, "And I love Daddy."
He puts his two year-old arms
round both their necks to hug them.
I marvel how he understands his bliss,
then run back out into the woods.

## Strange Fruits

*for Jenny*

Few could conceive of venturing out after dark,
forehead glowing in the murk like a deep-sea diver,
and swimming patiently the length of the lawn,
pot and stick in hand to harvest the ripening beasts
that appear from deep in the undergrowth to feed.

Yet there's an acquired taste that comes with surveying
the most intimate corners of the night-time garden –
the meeting of Woodlice, the greeting of Earwigs;
being for the Moths a mini-lunar magnet; and
stooping low over Lettuce seedlings, the strange

acrobats I spy hanging – brown Berthas with orange frills;
and curling from the ravaged Mizuna, soft cream slippers,
tortoiseshell buns, and the sleek, black moustaches
that are the heavy-weights of this night-time circus –
each persuaded from its perch and gathered

for displacement in a far-flung hedge or field.
Hearing of my nocturnal excursions, you extol the sheer
convenience of killing – the pellets you leave like grey scat
beside the Lupins.  Still our Birds find their fruits wherever
they fall, and isn't it the dead that taste strangest of all?

## The Japanese Madonna

As Madonna of Akita
I was carved
by a Buddhist from
a weeping katsura.

I forsook kimono and zori
for an unpainted robe,
a European chin,
and an aristocrat's gaze.

I dropped blood-tears,
my sweat stank of roses,
and I warned that fire
would fall from the sky.

In Ballinspittle
I was made of stone;
I just flexed my fingers
and rocked.

*Nuala Ni Chonchuir*

## Sofa

I squat by a farm-gate like a sneaky pisser,
hunched low, arms bent, wearing ruin heavily.

Domestic glories are gone: no more coin caches,
scattered plumpy cushions, or copulating couples.

My lap is torn velour that belches foam and springs
around arse-shaped dinges and unnameable stains.

But despite being careworn, I am still useful:
my insides are a womb to a mischief of mice.

## Miscarriage and Dream

When I looked at the snow-field screen
Where you were helplessly *sous neige,*
I knew I would see only a static curl.
My heart slowed to breaking, to match yours,
Stopped.
That night, the Virgin statue came to life,
And took your unformed body in her hands,
She popped you in her mouth, and smiled.

## Pinteresque in Portrush

There is silence
as we enter the dining room.

Middle-aged couples
twitch uncomfortably,
taking breakfast
a marriage apart.

Outside, rain falls
as if it always does;
inside, the day is
overcast, outlook bleak.

Miss Robinson is
a terrifying, presiding
presence. Her authority
is worn heavy as a cloak.

No weasel would
dare reside beneath
the cocktail cabinet
she would never possess.

We pause; breathe
deeply; take our seats.

*Jeremy Page*

# Shaving my Father

He once taught me the art –
how the badger hair brush,
soap bowl and Wilkinson Sword blade
combined to render smooth
the contours of my chin,
to shear those first few stalks
scattered unconvincingly, apologetically
across my teenage features;
and did this with some reluctance
as if, with the shaven hairs,
I'd wash away my childhood
and all that meant to me, to him.
Tomorrow he may not know
who I am or who I was,
but today he does, and is grateful
for the care I take
as I soap his face
with the badger hair brush,
move the blade gently down his chin,
hear his stubble crack.

## Learning Irony

Nearly twenty years later,
our lives all petition and solicitor,
I discover the name of the hill
across the valley from where
we threw off our clothes
that first soft spring day
comes from the Welsh
for *divorce* or *separation*.

And now I see the irony,
but then there was none,
just you and me on a hillside
under the vault of heaven,
making something like love.
At least, our passion spent,
it was upwards we stared
and not across to Skirrid.

## Time of Rosellas

*Zimbabwe 2007*

There are three rooms.
She chooses the bricks, the tiles, the proportions.
He chooses the one with a bed, a chair

there's no mirror, he's grown old
without knowing. Outside, sun
bakes the high walls.

And among the mopani trees,
where a yellow and black tortoise
shuffles butterfly leaves,

he waits for the time of rosellas,
spreads maize cobs to dry flat
on a garden's red earth

to keep them safe from the men
who will rob, who are new;
orders her dogs gently in Shona

as he walks them on kopjes
where stories are told without words
in caves without date.

On a field overgrown with weeds,
a child stumbles, the infant tied to her back
tries to cry.

*Rosella: A tropical shrub with short-lived yellow flowers.
The fruit is made into jelly with a flavour of rose-hips.
Shona: The language of the Mashonaland people.
Kopje: A small natural hill.*

## Valentine's Day

*We called her Nyasha, it means mercy,*
the child-widow says, as she sees a land
where more than sun burns.

>           *There is suffering, man, plenty of suffering,*
>           the worshipper says, as the highveldt bleeds
>           into mounds of red earth.

*We love you. God bless the country we share,*
the farmer's wife says, as armed police stand by
on Valentine's Day.

>           *The snakes are in the water, not long now,*
>           the actor says, as a crowd starts to form
>           on the township street.

*Soon, it will be soon! Our seeds will grow tall,*
the brave man says, as the soldiers close in
with sjamboks and wire.

## Harare Song

*After Kurt Weill*

Dressed in white he's a presence
moving past open doors, padding
over mukwa floors he polishes daily
*yes, madam, things are very bad*
and twice-daily his wife returns
to breast-feed their baby

while flamboyants grace the sky
in the avenues of plenty like
blood umbrellas not trees. *Walk
slowly please, there's a guard
with a gun who is staring.*

At lights, fingers reach up to car windows
hold a cup. *Nobody gives money!*
But we do. *Ndatenda,* small hands
come together to clap, to give thanks
perhaps to pray before, bare-foot
the child runs away

while flamboyants grace the sky
in the avenues of plenty like
blood umbrellas not trees. *Walk
slowly please, there's a guard
with a gun who is staring.*

Wearing once khaki rags, matted hair
huge in unravelling hat, a man sits
detached from the queues, unconcerned.
*Gone,* you say, *he's out of it now.*
At the roadside bent women
plant mealies too late

while flamboyants grace the sky
in the avenues of plenty like
blood umbrellas not trees. *Walk
slowly please, there's a guard
with a gun who is staring.*

## Ladders Appear at Fences

Brick sheds diminish, brambles lift over walls
gardens give onto wasteland, feet into miles

espalier trees link arms around the yard –
there is always stuff to be thrown out, junked, denied –

removals heap into skips, the engines growl
cucumbers fatten in cold-frames, greenhouses boil

gutter-pipes reach up at corners, bins wait in line
washing flies sidewards away from the wind,

sorrell burns the embankment, rust on the rail
the mainline goes elsewhere, channelled to change

and footballs barge into bushes, newspapers fall,
breadcrumbs are scattered on patios, curtains are drawn

children are playing at houses, adults too late
tenants touch up their paintwork, cars on display

lorries heave onto motorways, distances lead
flowerheads open their hands, and windows swing free

aerials jostle for signals, the programmes come
and every departure engenders a home,

carrots emerge from allotments, plugs pull on drains
ladders appear at fences, people climb.

## Something Happens, Sometimes Here

From the open window plates clank into sinks.
Pampas grass, blue and sharp, thrusts a head.

Its rapiers wait, stiff with outrage
stuck in this dusty corner of rural Lincolnshire

home of lost causes and chimneypots.
A spindryer drones on down to a stuttering halt.

The River of Life Ministry proclaims God's kingdom
in faded handbills: *the wisdom of the wise is foolishness*

and: *Rottweiler puppy for sale, eight months old.*
A jet stripes its lonely line down the sky's big face.

It's Saturday, it's July, and nobody's out
the dance is cancelled, the caravans moved on

it's business as usual in silent towns
with window displays that haven't been changed

since the day the cinema was bombed in '44.
And junkyard houses march backwards

to green seas crested with kale, waterbutts, canes
the praiseworthy end of labours

and sheaves of Golden Rod. It's all in order, friends
your lives are pure there's nothing to reach you here

the kingdom is safe, the bunting flutters in peace
streaming from thick-legged architecture,

men will soon be home in their brylcreemed hair
your bakelite sets alive with plosive announcements....

I walk down a blind lane. Houses in curious brick,
tendrils escape from the sides of crumbling ledges.

Grade 1 viola floats past. A piano goes stumbling after,
playlist to How I Began. And somebody comes.

*Nick Pearson*

## Made in Captivity

Dolphins are the only animals
that really look like themselves
as souvenir models on a shelf:

shiny, plastic,
a neck-head umbilical plughole
where they were snatched wet
from a manufacturing process.

In the zoo shop
they densely fill three baskets –
baby, medium and large.
My hand churns their satisfying bulk.
Breed, breed, it says. Collect, collect.

Joan Poulson

## Alice B. Toklas cooks fish

My grandmother insisted that 'once caught,
fish should have nothing more to do with water'.

When Picasso came to lunch I simmered
dry white wine with blade mace,
a leaf from Apollo's laurel and herbs: thyme,
tarragon, rosemary; fresh torn,
earth and sun resonating through my body.

Later I laid a firm striped bass to poach,
removed it from the fire,
left it to cool in the *court-bouillon*.

My design? Inspired!
A satin coverlet of yellow mayonnaise:
eggs, green oil.
To amuse, with a pastry tube, I swirled
an extravagance of red cream,

not tainted with commercial colouring
but from my own paste –
tomatoes lusciously plumped with sun.

And then, cunning detail, sieved
hard-boiled eggs (whites, yolks
kept separate) and truffles finely sliced.
A final touch – dusting of *fines herbes*
with, my own conceit, basil.
I was proud of my *chef d'oeuvre*.

*Incroyable!* Picasso exclaimed
as Helene brought it to table
but Gertrude rocked in silent mirth
when, inflexion of eyebrow perfect-pitched,
that one murmured that it might rather
have been sculpted in honour of Matisse.

## Snow

first the surprise of it, the odd delight
a fluke Diwali cold-snap and suddenly
great globs of bright are spiralling

running the gauntlet to do the bins
I'm caught out by the floodlight infrared,
it turns the fall to magic cuts of mirror ball

and I am spinning, calling you to see
the fractal clumps that rest then melt
on my tongue's tip, like things unsaid

and so it settles, blanketing our cars
paired up like shoes as we nuzzle up
and you decide to, after all, stay over

as night begins to freeze us in
the powder-soft reveals its crystal heart
and slips from dancing flakes to static ice

I start to dread the inconvenience

*Pauline Suett Barbieri*

## Thinking of my Mum While Studying an Etch of an Imaginary Prison by Giovanni Battista Piranesi

So often she is a book mark in my life.
For a moment, sentenced between the black and white
                                        brandishment
of swirling pulley ropes, knotted braids of screams
and rat like stones smashing down onto a crumbling floor.

She could tell him something about prison.
About how it was as a girl, in a convent,
finding herself pregnant with a Protestant man's child.
How iron fisted gates clamped down in front of them,

locking in life, pushing them both towards the rack,
ready to be hung, drawn and quartered.
How she stood her ground, halted the rope around dad's neck,
looping it over a threadbare heart. Love's warden,

calling in the guise of a priest, Father O'Malley, offering
                                        crumbs
of forgiveness, pushing them through a Judas hole.
Dad repenting with love, took another faith back to the war.
                                        Crossing himself,
he managed to heave a carved head of shame out of one cell

into another. Piranesi standing high on a cracked abutment
reminds Rome what love is about. Restores passion.
Married in October, 'forty one', the rusty ring passing
                                              between them
recently loosened from an ankle chain in the 'Round Tower'.

*Pauline Suett Barbieri*

## Portrait of the Artist's Wife

When she arrived home she found
the bedroom had changed into a blank canvas
and the tap in the bathroom dripping his favourite oil
colour; burnt sienna. She could hardly open the door,
a gooey mess straddled the carpet.
She had no turps to thin it down.
As she tried to palette the mess, the colour
turned to cadmium orange; her favourite.
It started to lick her ankles, coat her legs.
It was just outlining her knees
when emerald green spluttered out,
spraying her new designer suit. She swore.
But then it looked more appealing
so when ultramarine started flowing
the colour of her eyes, she let it
swathe her shoulders and connect to their base.
Finally she managed to close the tap.
Suddenly the other tap opened, sprayed
egg-shell varnish over her new hairdo. She swore again.
The door opened and her sleepy-eyed husband
came in and nailed her to the wall.

*Kay Syrad*

## Letter from my brother

When I saw those words a goose flew into my chest
and beat its wings in there, and there was laughing

on the other side, where all the chickens, the litters,
were scrambling up the sides and down, on the grass,

falling over each other in their innocence. Fresh-daisy
excitement! The sun beating down on our heads,

the laughing, the beach huts, the long promenade
with the huge round pebbles below, the wind, the light-

grey of the sea wall and the suck of that wind, pulling
our faces into smiles, smiling itself; the stripes, awning,

rain – and always the laughter, incessant, long—ours.
Our show, our imagined world, the singing, chancing,

and everywhere the awning. We were stiff as frost,
folded, stacked, but the breath on the glass was ours.

*Simon Williams*

## By Rail

Outside Reigate,
as the train slows for a signal,
there's a fox, as sharp as ginger,
standing guard by the slope of ballast.

9:30, bright June, as travellers
from Gatwick remember Alicante,
the dog fox doesn't flinch
or turn for cover.

The vixen,
curled behind him
like a terrier by the fire,
lifts her head to check he's there.

That's all the Reading train,
formed of three coaches, allows;
two seconds' worth of fox,
two seconds from a forward-facing seat.

## Epidauros

When a man whispers at that focus,
swears under his breath,
appeals to a woman to turn and look,
those words are heard right up to the cavea.
He speaks to every woman in the place,
curses the whole audience,
as if standing nose-to-nose
with the biggest and quickest to anger.

Every semi-circle in the auditorium
rises over the heads a row in front,
so everyone can see you, too;
ten thousand meet you eye-to-eye,
stare you down, weep for you.
Who wouldn't be an actor at that point?

*Hilary Willmott*

**Bubbles**

As she bathed that morning
they popped and fizzed around her

As she spread them across her breasts
their indecipherable discourse continued

As she stood to dry herself they sang
unperturbed by her departure

As the water drained beneath them
they lingered on, soaking in her DNA

As she dressed, they became a tighter group
popping and fizzing harmoniously

As the front door opened the rush of air gave power
to their voices, which chorused a carbonated au revoir

As she lay lifeless in the road, hair still damp
they became sotto voce, hesitant

As if they knew the solemnity of the moment
and had adjusted their timbre accordingly

## Horse Sense

Where we've stopped to watch,
the paddock gate's seasoned
with a sprinkling of hoar,
the ground's indurated with cold
and I'm holding you up to look,
remarking that today, even horses
are wearing their coats.
Your brow furrows for a moment,
before you ask how they put them on?
I can see the problem –
despite shoulder, elbow and knee
on the same limb, fetlock and pastern;
an abundance of joints which you'd think
made it possible to manoeuvre the aperture
in the cover over their heads; without hands
the praxis would obviously be difficult –
and we don't believe in magic.

I can only suggest that the horse
hoofs out the material on the field,
as if unrolling a carpet, and then
taking two corners (one by one) in its mouth,
carefully folds it along a central crease.
Bringing the front sides of the garment

into apposition, and leaving sufficient space
for its head to pass through, it nudges
the collar into existence, compressing
the top margins (that must be made
of Velcro or have magnets sewn in the hem)
with a patting movement of its nose.
Then with an almighty kick,
it tosses the whole thing into the air,
exhaling hot gas through dilated nostrils
sufficient to produce a brief lift,
at the same time executing a capriole,
aiming itself as precisely as possible
at the neck-hole, like a footballer
leaping to head a goal. No doubt
several attempts are necessary,
and once having got the coat
on its back, some minor adjustments
brought about by extreme lateral flexion
of the cervical region, enabling the collar
to be seized by the jaws and pulled forward.

We could imagine another method
that involves spreading the sheet out,
quickly doing a kind of Fosbury Flop

and somehow finishing legs up,
as if having a nappy changed;


then rubbling or shuffling along the ground
in such a way as to make the cloth
adhere to the dorsum, before springing off,
and in mid-air, clasping the neckpiece
together with the under-surface of the hooves
– but this seems implausible.

*Michael  J.Woods*

## A Bluebell From St Bueno's

Weary after a long term we drove to Wales –
your world for a while where *springs not fail*.
After the study session at the *Bod Eryn* Hotel
we tucked into pied beauty for lunch –
trout and almonds, chips with a twist of lemon.
We traced our way over your pastoral forehead,
the turrets of St. Beuno's set square
against the Vale of Clwyd.

Not the right thing to do, perhaps
but I picked a flower that went to press.
What you might have said to me about
my act of stealth as I slipped the bluebell
between the passions of your poems
I know I'll never know but, since then,
veins have been visibly bound, fastened
to a page that's almost the colour of flesh.

## Kevin de Medici

Uncle Lorenzo really pisses me off.
*The Magnificent*, they call him. He owns almost all of
Florence
Cosimo, my dad, says he'll get his hands on the lot one day.
He's always at the office; that's not my scene.

I hang out with a happening crowd.
We meet under David's dick,
sometimes drive out to Fiesole and frighten nuns.
Orsino, the arsehole, says it could become a habit.
I told him, said I couldn't see a future for me in banking.
Yes, we're loaded but the medici.co.it
bubble has to burst sometime.

Dad tarts about with poofs like Micky Angelo,
got him to paint my bedroom ceiling last year.
Mum had a makeover for the lounge thrown in.

I've got a bit of a racket going with the gold
traders on the Ponte Vecchio. The butchers
don't like it but I'm first violin around here

I've enrolled for a GNVQ in Leisure and Tourism.
I'm far sighted, see. Scrapping  between nation states is crap,
has to stop sometime. All that shit between

                         Guelphs and Ghibellines

lost us Dante. Absolute pants, eh?

I've asked Mick to knock out some cardboard cut-outs
of D and B to flog on the bridge. If they go well, the next

                                       caper

will be T-shirts. Next? Well, I'm working with a mate
from Venice. Glarse souvenirs bust easy. I can't wait.

## Windhover Bovver

*Gerard Manley Hopkins Writes to R.B in Cockney Slang*

Cream-crackered after me mornin' prayers,
out the window I clocked this 'awk – a bird
climbin' the apples 'n' pears o' the air.
Gor blimey! Would you Adam 'n' Eve it?
I'm searchin' me gravy train for a word
to celebrate the little sod's achieve
ment – when it buggered off! I was in stress,
lookin' f'me bird book – but no success.
Then I remembered. Young Felix Randal
borrowed it just before 'e popped 'is clogs…
No one else I've met could 'old a candle
to 'im. This country's goin' to the dogs.
Yours, *Gezza*. P.S. This Easter bonnet
should buckle under what the ac's write on it.